1

Franklin has a problem

Houses are very different. Some are
huge and have gold swimming pools.
Pop stars live in those. Some are in
rows with a brick wall at one end and
overlook a pie factory. Franklin Gates
lives in one of those. Number three,
Stanley Street, to be exact.

Some people might think, 'I want a
house with a swimming pool.' But not
Franklin.

He loved living on Stanley Street. Everyone was friendly. All his mates were there and the smells from the pie factory … mmm, delicious! There was just one problem. Franklin's mum and dad wanted to move. His mum was expecting twins and they needed another bedroom.

'I don't mind sharing mine,' Franklin said.

'Babies cry all night.'

'I'll wear earplugs.'

But his parents wouldn't listen.

'This house is TOO small,' said his mum.

Next day, there was a 'For Sale' sign stuck by Franklin's door.

Franklin and his best friend Josh stared at the words of doom.

'What am I going to do, Josh?' said Franklin.

Josh frowned. 'Has your house got problems? Number forty's got problems and no one wants to buy it.'

Franklin stared at number forty. It looked all right to him. 'What kind of problems?' he asked.

'Oh, mice and damp and really horrible wallpaper.'

Franklin sighed. His house was warm and friendly and it had just been painted, worse luck.

Mrs Cox lived next door to Franklin in a little house that had once been the corner shop. Just then, she called out, 'Hello, lads. Will you take ...'

Before she could finish, her dog Zack leaped out of her house.

He jumped up at the boys, trying to lick their faces.

'Yuk! Down, Zack!' Josh giggled.

Mrs Cox told Zack to get down. 'He hasn't been out all day. I've been a bit wobbly,' she said, tapping her legs.

'No worries,' Franklin smiled. He didn't mind taking Zack anywhere. He loved him to bits.

'I'm sorry you're moving,' Mrs Cox said.

'So am I,' Franklin grumbled.

Mrs Cox patted Franklin on the arm. 'Never mind. Your house might take months to sell.'

For a week, it looked as if Mrs Cox was right. Only a few people came to look at the house and none of them wanted to buy it. Franklin's mum stroked her growing tummy and looked fed up.

Upstairs, Franklin danced around with his underpants on his head in celebration. Maybe he was safe. Maybe no one would buy his house.

But a few days later – it must have been Thursday, because the smells from the pie factory were chicken and rhubarb – Franklin came home from school to find a man in the kitchen. His name was Mr Bragg and was interested in buying the house.

Mr Bragg *wasn't* interested in Franklin. He glared at Franklin and trod on his toes, without saying sorry.

Franklin's heart sank when Mr Bragg said he wanted to come back for a second visit.

'Saturday morning, ten o'clock sharp,' he said.

2

Franklin makes a plan

That night, Franklin had a bad dream. Mr Bragg was sniggering at him, 'You wait and see, boy. *I'm* going to have your house!'

Then Franklin woke up. 'No, you won't, you tatty toe-cruncher!' he said angrily.

At school, Franklin asked Josh what he was doing on Saturday.

Josh shrugged. 'Nothing much.'

'Does your big sister still work in the fish shop?' asked Franklin.

Josh nodded.

'Good. Listen, I've got a job for you …'

Franklin cupped his hand over Josh's ear and began whispering his plan.

When Josh heard what Franklin wanted, his mouth opened wide enough to swallow a dentist. 'I can't do that!' he cried. 'I'll get into trouble!'

'You have to! It's my only chance,' Franklin begged.

In the end, Josh nodded. He wasn't happy, but he agreed to do what Franklin wanted.

3

Something is fishy

On Saturday morning, Franklin's mum
was in a flap. 'Something smells horrible
and I don't know what it is,' she said.
She looked around in a panic. 'Your
dad's outside checking the drains.'

Franklin smiled. He knew what the
smell was!

Mr and Mrs Gates were still outside
when Mr Bragg rang the doorbell.
Franklin let him into the house.

Mr Bragg stopped and sniffed the air. 'Ugh, what's that disgusting smell?' he asked.

'It's Saturday. The factory does fish pie on Saturdays,' Franklin said.

Mr Bragg frowned. 'Isn't the factory shut on Saturdays?'

'No. Fish every Saturday. That's why we call this Stinky Street. D'you want to see my bedroom?'

Upstairs, Franklin opened his bedroom door. Mr Bragg pointed to a huge, dark patch on the wall. 'What's that?' he asked.

'Damp,' Franklin said. 'Mum made me cover it with a poster last time.'

'Hmm,' Mr Bragg snorted.

'Mind the mouse poo,' Franklin grinned, pointing to a pile of brown lumps. 'It gets stuck in the carpet.'

'Urgh!' Mr Bragg pulled a face.

'That's nothing,' smiled Franklin.
'Wait till you see what the rats do,'

At that moment, his mum arrived.
'Hello,' she smiled. 'How's it going?'

'Your son was telling me about the
rats,' Mr Bragg said, icily.

'Rats? What rats …'

'Oh, no!' Franklin yelled, pointing
out of the window.

'What is it?' asked Mr Bragg.

'That horrible Josh Barratt's coming! Quick! Hide!' yelled Franklin.

'Hide from Josh? Don't be silly,' Franklin's mum said. But Franklin ducked behind his curtains.

'Josh is a lovely boy!' Franklin's mum said, amazed.

But Josh banged on the front door. He shouted football songs. He even burped through the letterbox.

'Why you little …' Mr Bragg gasped as Josh ran off.

'Er … would you like to see the bathroom?' Mrs Gates asked, but Mr Bragg shook his head.

'You're joking. I'm not staying here another minute.'

He ran downstairs and out of the door.

4

Mrs Cox joins in

Mr and Mrs Gates were very angry. 'You'd better explain what's going on!' they told Franklin.

'Er … well … I –'

Just then, there was a loud banging.

'It's coming from Mrs Cox's house,' Franklin's mum said, glaring at her son. 'Fancy getting an old lady mixed up in this!'

'I didn't,' Franklin cried. 'I really didn't!'

The banging grew louder and louder. Then Zack started barking. Something was very wrong.

Mr and Mrs Gates and Franklin dashed into Mrs Cox's house.

She was lying by her stairs, where she had tripped. Franklin helped his dad lift her carefully onto a chair. Mr Gates wanted to take her to hospital but Mrs Cox wouldn't go.

'I'm not leaving Zack,' she said. So they rang her son Eric, and he came to help her.

Mrs Cox was safe but Franklin knew he was still in big trouble. He ran back home and took the fish out of the back of the radiator. (Josh's sister had given it to him.)

He vacuumed up the chocolate drops on the carpet in his bedroom.

Then he dried the lemonade on his bedroom wall. He said sorry to Josh for getting him into trouble, too. At last, he said sorry to his mum and dad. His mum was very upset.

'We know you love Stanley Street. We all do –'

'– But there won't be space for all of us, when the twins arrive,' his dad said firmly. 'We have got to move to a bigger house.'

'I know,' Franklin said, sadly.

Weeks passed but no one came to look at the house. Winter was coming and Franklin began to feel hopeful. Nobody wanted to move in winter, did they?

But one day, Franklin came home from school to find creepy Mr Bragg in the kitchen again. He'd found out about Franklin's tricks and he still wanted their house.

'Those Gates have got to move,' Mr Bragg said to himself. 'I'll get their house cheap!' He smiled slyly and gave Franklin's mum a piece of paper with a price on it. It was a very low price.

'Let me know tomorrow if I can buy it,' Mr Bragg smirked. 'Make up your mind. No one else wants it.'

'We'll think about it,' Mrs Gates said, going pale.

'Do we have to sell to HIM?' Franklin cried as soon as he'd gone.

'I expect so,' said his mum.

Franklin was furious. How *could* his mum and dad sell to Mr Bragg?

Even the delicious smell of lamb and bananas coming from the pie factory didn't help. 'I'm going to take Zack for a run,' Franklin said. 'A long run. To Scotland.'

'Oh, dear,' said his mum.

Mrs Cox took ages to answer the door. She was even slower on her feet since her fall.

'I was coming round to your house!'
Mrs Cox beamed. 'Is your mum in? I've
got something to ask her.'

'Yes,' said Franklin. He was trying to
stop being licked to bits by Zack.

'Bring him back by tea time,' Mrs Cox
called as he set off with the dog.

'I will,' Franklin said.

'I was talking to Zack,' Mrs Cox joked.

When Franklin came back, Mrs Cox
was just leaving his house. 'How was
Scotland?' she joked.

'Cold,' said Franklin, crossly.

Mrs Cox laughed as if he'd cracked the funniest joke ever. 'You'd better get inside and warm up, then,' she told him, grinning.

Franklin felt grumpy. 'I don't know why Mrs Cox thinks moving house is so funny …' He stopped. His mum was dancing round the room with – yes – underpants on her head! 'What's going on?' he asked.

'Wait and see!' she laughed.

It was Christmas time in Stanley Street. There was no 'For Sale' sign outside Franklin's house. Instead, there were piles of bricks and cement from the builders.

'That was a great idea of Mrs Cox's,' Josh said. 'You bought her house and knocked both of your houses together –'

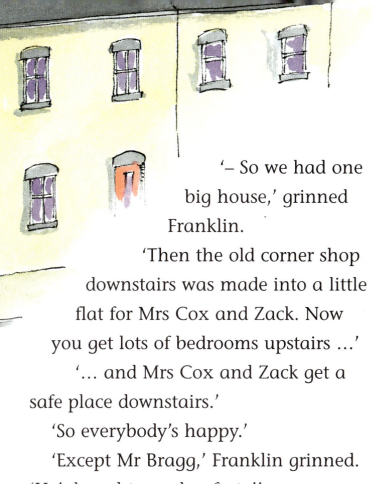

'– So we had one big house,' grinned Franklin.

'Then the old corner shop downstairs was made into a little flat for Mrs Cox and Zack. Now you get lots of bedrooms upstairs …'

'… and Mrs Cox and Zack get a safe place downstairs.'

'So everybody's happy.'

'Except Mr Bragg,' Franklin grinned. 'He's bought number forty!'

About the author

Stanley Street is a real street near where I live in Nottinghamshire. It is the only street of houses in the middle of an industrial estate full of do-it-yourself stores and carpet warehouses and car showrooms.

It seems a strange place for a row of old houses, and I often wonder about the people who live there. Sadly, there isn't a pie factory like in my story or I'd live there myself!

Lincolnshire
COUNTY COUNCIL

discover libraries

This book should be returned on or before the last date shown below. MD2

19 AUG 2023

05
2 8 AUG 2023

To renew or order library books please telephone 01522 782010
or visit www.lincolnshire.gov.uk

You will require a Personal Identification Number.
Ask any member of staff for this.

04887512